Tintorett

S. L. Bensusan

(Editor: T. Leman Hare)

Alpha Editions

This edition published in 2023

ISBN : 9789362098467

Design and Setting By
Alpha Editions
www.alphaedis.com
Email - info@alphaedis.com

PLATE I.—A KNIGHT OF MALTA.
Frontispiece (From Hampton Court)

This portrait (note the Maltese crosses on the cloak) is a splendid example of Tintoretto's gifts as a portrait painter. It should be remembered that three or four hundred years have helped the restorer's arts to spoil much of the painter's work.

I

Sometime in the second decade of the sixteenth century there was born to one Battista Robusti, cloth-dyer of Venice, a boy to whom the name Jacopo was given. We know nothing of the childhood of the lad who, because his father's business was that of a "tintore" or dyer, was known to his companions as Tintoretto. But one, Carlo Ridolfi, who was born about the time when Tintoretto died, towards the close of the sixteenth century, tells us that the "little dyer," whose name is written so large in the history of sixteenth-century art, started very early to practise drawing, and used his father's working material in order to give his productions the colour they seemed to need. That he must have shown signs of uncommon talent at an early age is shown by the fact that he found his way to the studio or workshop of Titian, the greatest painter in the Venice of his time; a man whose position enabled him to require, from all who sought to become his pupils, a measure of proficiency that promised to make their work useful when the demands of patrons were more than one painter could hope to satisfy unaided. Only the lad who possessed undeniable gifts or powerful patrons could find a place in the workshop of the greatest painter of the day, and Tintoretto was quite without patronage. The story-tellers of the period assure us that pupil and master quarrelled, they even hint that Titian was jealous of the young student, and this of course is not impossible because we have plenty of instances on record in which jealousy has been found thriving within the studio. Then, again, clever lads are not always tactful, and an unbridled tongue may make hosts of enemies, and destroy the atmosphere of repose in which alone good work is possible. A brilliant painter might well have been a little intolerant of precocious pupils.

Entering into detail, Ridolfi tells us in his life of the painter that when Tintoretto was at work in Titian's studio he copied some of the master's pictures so cleverly that Titian told one of his other pupils to send the boy away, and Robusti was dismissed from the studio without explanation. It is a significant fact, at the service of those who accept the theory of jealousy, that throughout the years when Tintoretto was struggling for recognition Titian had no eyes for his young pupil's work, and was only led to praise a picture by seeing it unsigned and exhibited in the open. There were times when the elder painter could have placed commissions in the young man's way, but he seems to have preferred to help others, of whom Paolo Cagliari, known as the Veronese, is the only man whose work retains a large place in the public eye. But clearly Titian must have had some other motive as well as jealousy, for he himself had more work than he could possibly do, and the help of a clever pupil like Tintoretto would have been valuable in times of great stress when patrons were waxing impatient. Whatever the other motive may have been it escaped Ridolfi, and no other record of the early days is extant.

PLATE II.—THE DOGE ALVISE MOCENIGO

This portrait, to be seen to-day in the Accademia at Venice, is one of the most striking of the long series of the leading citizens of the Republic. Tintoretto painted many of these portraits, for he was for many years one of the official painters to the Republic. Venice holds the best of this work.

Looking at the work of the "little dyer" it seems reasonable to suggest that he acted as all great painters before and after him have done—that is to say, he sought what was best in the work around him, and having collected all the material he required, evolved his own artistic personality from a judicious selection. Artists do not come into this world ready made, and the period of the making depends upon the man. For many, life is not long enough, and it is one of the tragedies of art work that the mastery over technical difficulties is sometimes delayed until the eye is becoming dim and the hand uncertain. From the very first we find that Tintoretto was immersed in the affairs of his art, that he could not hold his hand, that he laboured with feverish energy, that no commission was despised, and that nothing was too large or too small for him to undertake. Throughout the days of his youth his industry was devoted entirely to mastering the difficult technique of his work, until foreshortening, perspective, correct anatomy, relative values, light, shadow, and relief, were his subjects rather than his masters. Then he was prepared to begin where so many great Venetian artists had left off.

It had been a reproach to the Venetians that for all their colour they were poor draughtsmen. Needless to add that this rebuke came from the schools of Florence, where men were more concerned with correct drawing than rich colour. But Tintoretto removed the reproach from Venice, and, while he learned to draw in fashion that left the Florentine schools nothing to teach, he followed Gian Bellini and Titian into the domain of colour, and his work to-day reveals many of the best qualities of the two Italian schools of art in happy combination. When he was fully equipped according to his lights, and was prepared to enter into competition with the men around him, Tintoretto set out boldly to achieve the best results—he knew what he could do even if he did not know what the accomplishment was worth. It was not a part of his mental attitude to rest content with work done for those who sought the service of second-class men. "The form of Michelangelo, the colour of Titian;" these were the achievements he sought to realise, and he wrote these words on the wall of his workshop in the same spirit as that in which pious Hebrews still put the declaration of their faith upon the doorposts of their houses. He understood that Michelangelo Buonarotti had said the last word in form, and that Titian had gone as far in the direction of colour. Not until he was armed with patiently acquired skill, extraordinary natural aptitude, and a temperament that could not be satisfied with anything less than complete success, did he feel prepared to take the world of art by storm, and then he had put to the credit of his record a measure of hard work that no other painter could show.

For the first few years Tintoretto had to strive in the ranks of men who, whatever their gifts, had more chances than he. Venice was full of artists; commissions did not always depend upon merit, influence and favour counted for a great deal, and the clever son of an obscure dye-worker could hardly reach the goal of his ambitions without a long period of waiting. Things had altered from the days when Titian came from the mountains of Cadore to the studio of Gian Bellini, there was now so much talent in Venice that a man might have good gifts and yet go hungry. Art had widened its boundaries, developed the importance of its expression and the scope of its appeal, offering wealth and reputation to those who could succeed in impressing the statesman, churchman, or conqueror who held the patronage of the arts to be one of the special privileges of their state.

In Florence the tendency was to treat art as one branch of the many-sided profession of life. The artist of the day was sculptor and architect as well; sometimes he was engineer and statesman, he took every field of activity for his labours, and certainly the success of the great men whose range of endeavour was so wide was quite remarkable. Happily the Venetians were less ambitious. Bellini, who is, in the colour sense, the father of Venetian art, had a comparatively restricted outlook. Titian, his pupil, went farther afield and divorced art from the church, doubtless Giorgione had he lived would have helped to make that divorce more effective. Tintoretto, who was Titian's pupil, just as Titian had been Bellini's, was content to give all his energies, his extraordinary industry, and his great gifts to the service of painting. He could not enlarge the boundaries because Titian had carried them already into the domain of mythology, allegory, and portrait painting, and the time had not yet come when landscape could stand by itself. But Tintoretto, though he could not develop the theme, managed to develop the treatment, and became in a sense to be discussed later on the "father" of impressionism. This was his special service to art, and must be regarded as a remarkable discovery when we see how firmly fixed were the ordinary painters' conventions in handling subjects. Titian had broken away from the restrictions on subject matter, it was left to Tintoretto to revolt against the conventional handling, but this revolt was of course the product of late years. He began where his masters were leaving off, and he ended by being a law to himself. It will be seen, judging by the statements of his biographers, and particularly that of Ridolfi to whom we have referred, that the young painter's gifts and his habit of thinking for himself and following his theories into the realm of practice were in the way of his advancement. He worked so rapidly that the people to whom he applied in the first instance for commissions were a little suspicious. They could not understand how a man who painted with lightning rapidity and was prepared to sell his labour for any price, however small, could claim to be taken seriously. His cleverness made them afraid. They do not seem to have understood the type of artist that works because work is the very first law of life, and is content with a small return, knowing that when once the proper chance has come it will be possible to command a better price.

PLATE III.—THE ORIGIN OF "THE MILKY WAY"

This extraordinary painting to be seen to-day at the National Gallery reveals not only the artist's vivid imagination but the wonderful skill with which he can present a flying figure and leave it as though supported in mid air. Students of Tintoretto will not fail to note the resemblance between the flying figure here and the one in "The Miracle of the Slave" in the Venetian Academy.

The general feeling about Jacopo Robusti is perhaps summed up by Giorgio Vasari in his "Lives." "He is a great lover of the arts," says our gossip; "he delights in playing on various musical instruments; he is a very agreeable person, but as far as painting is concerned he has the most capricious hand, and the boldest, most extravagant, and most obstinate brain that ever belonged to painter. Of this the proof lies in his works and in their fantastic composition so different from the usage of other painters. Indeed, Robusti becomes more than ever extravagant in his recent inventions, and the strange fancies that he has executed as it were almost without design, as though he aimed to show that art is but a jest. He will sometimes present as finished, sketches which are just such mere outlines that the spectator sees before him pencil marks made by chance, the result of a bold carelessness rather than the fruits of design and judgment."

These are significant words only when we consider that they were written at a time when Tintoretto was alive, and Vasari must have been moved to great excess of zeal to have gone so far in the painter's dispraise. Indeed he closes his little sketch by remarking that Tintoretto after all is a very clever man and a highly commendable painter. The special interest of the criticism lies in its revelation of the attitude of his contemporaries towards Tintoretto. For more than a century art had been moving, pictures had ceased to be flat, the difficulties of chiaroscuro were being faced rather than shirked. Atmosphere was growing, the problems of perspective were deemed worthy of careful study. Colour was not only brilliant, but the secret of mixing colours long since lost and apparently irrecoverable was known in the studios of the leading men. But the very earliest lessons of impressionism had yet to be taught, and realism had rendered dull and lifeless pictures that were hung rather beyond the reach of the spectator's close scrutiny. Tintoretto saw that work must be handled in such a fashion that the spectator who stood some distance away could get an impression of the whole of the subject treated. He knew that if objects were painted with equal values and the meticulous care of the miniaturist the canvas would only yield its fruit to those who could stare right into it. These facts were a pleasant revelation to him and an unpleasant one to his contemporaries. His work was destined to influence Velazquez—Velazquez influenced Goya, the mantle of Goya fell upon Edouard Manet, and Manet founded the great impressionist school of France that has been doing work of extraordinary merit and enduring interest while schoolmen of contemporary generations have been concerned with telling stories in terms of paint and harking back to the pre-Raphaelities.

The modern work suffers more from neglect and disregard than that of the great masters of old time, because nowadays it is possible to multiply the lowest and most popular class of picture and scatter it broadcast among those who have no knowledge of the aims and objects of art. They think that a picture is bound to be a good one if it should chance to appeal to them, forgetful that their lack of taste may have as much as anything to do with the appeal of the work. A picture may please an observer because the picture is great or because the observer is small, but the latter alternative is hardly popular with those who go conscientiously to galleries.

Vasari tells us many stories of Tintoretto's inexhaustible activity. Ridolfi does the same, and it is easy to understand why a man who could not keep his brush from his hand for any length of time, and would accept any price or any commission rather than remain idle, was rather a terror to his contemporaries, and earned the title of "Il Furioso" by which he was widely known. Few artists in the world's history have achieved so much, for although we know of countless frescoes and pictures that have perished utterly, we still have something like six hundred works left to stand for the seventy-five years of the painter's life, and some of these, such as the works in the Doges' Palace, are crowded with figures. Indeed the work in the Doges' Palace might well stand for the life's monument of any artist however long-lived and industrious.

It is no fault of Tintoretto that his work baffles the tired eye. He cannot be studied in a day, or two days, or even three; you cannot go to him from other painters. He demands the closest and most enduring attention together with some expert guidance on the occasion of the first visit in order that the countless points in crowded canvas may not be overlooked. He was a man of such breadth of vision, his conceptions were so magnificent that he must be approached with something akin to reverence. We cannot go to him as to Titian or Bellini and feel that we can bring to the merit of each canvas the necessary amount of appreciation. While the "Paradiso" took years to complete, some of Tintoretto's smaller canvases took many months in the making, although the painter has never been excelled in the rapidity of execution. He who hopes to digest in half-an-hour the work that took Tintoretto half a year imagines a vain thing. To read some of the criticism that has been meted out to Tintoretto is to realise that their own limitations have given serious trouble to some of his critics, because he is so vast and so splendid in his themes, and so extraordinarily brilliant in his treatment, he has baffled one generation after another. His theory of relative values has been misunderstood and misinterpreted, but to see him in his true light it is necessary to consider how many of his successors could paint a large figured picture on anything approaching the same scale with an equal measure of intelligence. Nowadays we do not look for heroic achievement; and it is perhaps as well, seeing that there is none to be had.

PLATE IV.—ST. GEORGE AND THE DRAGON

(National Gallery, London)

This remarkable work is one of the finest examples of Tintoretto in England. Composition and colouring are alike masterly and though some of the beauty of paint has passed, the St. George and the Dragon remains a striking work.

II

Thanks to Carlo Ridolfi we can form a fairly correct idea of the conditions under which young Tintoretto lived in the early days. The expulsion from Titian's studio must have been a very serious blow to his hopes and ambitions, but he did not repine unduly—he was made of sterner stuff. He took a small apartment and began those unremitting labours that were to land him in the first rank of draughtsmen. Through Daniele da Volterra, a pupil of Michaelangelo, he secured the models of the master's work that were to teach him so much about anatomy, and were to be used for experiments in foreshortening, and the treatment of light and shade. He had one friend, an artist known as Schiavone, a man almost as poor as himself in those first days of struggle and disappointment—a man who had likewise sought instruction in Titian's studio but had left it without incurring that great master's ill-will. One of the earliest commissions that fell to Schiavone was for the decoration of St. Mark's Library, but Tintoretto had to wait longer for work, and some years would seem to have passed before he realised his ambition and received a commission to paint altar-pieces. There are some workers to whom enforced idleness would be fatal, and Tintoretto might have been one of them, but for the fact that he had no capacity for indolence, and would work even though he worked for nothing.

The first church to give him a commission would seem to be that of Santa Maria del Carmine, and the impression that he gave to his masters must have been a very favourable one, for we find that the churches of St. Benedetto and Santo Spirito gave him orders soon after. Then the Scuola della Trinita recognised his talent, and gave him an order for certain pictures, including the famous "Death of Abel" and the equally famous "Adam and Eve," of which John Ruskin said, "this in absolute power of painting is the supremest work in all the world." These Scuoli or confraternities were both wealthy and powerful bodies, able and eager to give valuable commissions to artists. They would often grant permanent pay and regular work to the man whose accomplishment satisfied their requirements, and the work that remains to us shows that the directors of the Scuoli were men of taste and discretion.

As soon as Tintoretto felt that he was within sight of the goal of his ambitions he married, choosing for his wife one Faustina of Vescovi, the daughter of a patrician house, and a woman who seems to have realised that her husband's devotion to the ideals of art were likely to make him a very bad business man. Like many of the wives of clever men she played the tyrant in matters that did not concern the studio, and the painter would seem to have evaded some of her regulations for his comfort by saying the thing that was not. We would not say that he originated the habit, but it is said to have become popular and traces of it are still found among husbands in the twentieth century.

Tintoretto took a house in the west end of Venice on the Fondamenta dei Mori overlooking Murano, and there he worked hard and lived simply. He must have been a man of engaging manner and amusing conversation, because Ridolfi has recorded many amusing little facts about him in his famous volume of biographies.

PLATE V.—THE PROCURATOR MOROSINI

(From the Venetian Academy)

This is another of Tintoretto's official pictures. The Procurator, a man whose singular dignity is not affected by his rather coarse and heavy features, is wearing beautiful robes that are now beginning to fade.

Clearly Tintoretto believed that Titian was his enemy, although we do not find that the younger man took any steps to demonstrate his ill-will. It would seem that many men who came to Tintoretto's studio could talk of nothing but Titian's virtues, and that this conversation tired the younger man, who at last put an end to the gossip very cleverly. He secured an incomplete canvas by Titian and painted a figure into it, then he sent the picture to the house of his friend Contarino, where the gossips who dabbled in literature and art were accustomed to assemble. All who saw the picture praised it to the skies, and when they had finished chattering Tintoretto remarked that the work they admired so much was painted partly by himself. Thereafter the gossips seem to have found some other topics of conversation, and Tintoretto was able to pursue his paths in peace without suffering from comparisons that must have been odious.

The painter's union was blessed with children, of whom his daughter Marietta was perhaps his favourite. Until she was fifteen years of age she used to accompany her father through Venice dressed as a boy. She learned a great deal from him, and became a portrait painter, dying some little time before her father, to his great grief. Some few of Tintoretto's remarks have come down to us. He is said to have held that black and white are the most beautiful colours, and with the record of this opinion it becomes curious to see in Tintoretto's pictures how the splendid colouring that was needed to express his work in the days when he was young grew more and more sombre as time passed on, until the dominant tone became the golden brown that is familiar to students of his pictures. As a young man he revelled in bright colours, but in middle and old age their charm passed. There is something very human about this attitude towards externals. Tintoretto placed a very great importance upon drawing, more importance indeed than any of the Venetians had placed upon it before his time. He thought very little of copies from the nude, being no believer in the beauty of the average nude form, and holding that the hand of the artist is necessary in order to express to the full the beauty that the lines of the body suggest. One pauses to wonder how he would have regarded Schopenhauer's criticism of the female form.

Tintoretto had two sons, who became his pupils when they were old enough; he was more fortunate in his family than was his great master and rival, and his home life would seem to have been a tranquil one, because we have learned from Vasari that he was a good musician, and played well on several instruments. Music does not flourish in unhappy homes. He could not have entertained as Titian did, because throughout his life he was a comparatively poor man, but he gathered round him some of the most interesting people in his native city and, with the exception of Titian and Aretino, all seemed to have been well pleased with him. Aretino, of course, being the greatest gossip of his century, could not keep his tongue quiet under any circumstances, and never hesitated to say an unpleasant thing as long as it had wit or humour. Tintoretto bore with his old master's factotum as long as he could, and then his patience giving out, invited him to the studio and proceeded to take his measure with a naked dagger, recording it as though he was going to paint a portrait. Aretino, who seems to have been an arrant coward, took the hint and controlled his unruly tongue. Perhaps he realised that it was unnecessary as well as unwise to provoke a man who asked for nothing better than to be allowed to spend his life in hard work free from interruption.

It is quite likely that Tintoretto's amazing gifts, together with his capacity for hard work, would have brought him very rapidly to the front, had not Titian been the pride of the Venetians, but while the great painter from Cadore dominated the City of the Lagoons no other man could hope to stand beside him, and certainly Tintoretto did not improve his own chances by his violent early search for work, and his startling offers to paint pictures of any size for any price. Inasmuch as he did not place a high value upon his own work, it was unreasonable to expect that his patrons would fall into the error of over-praising it. In setting a value upon their own work most men remember that they are sellers, nor is it the business of buyers to raise the price.

It is no easy task to hunt out Tintoretto's countless pictures in Venice. Including panels, altar-pieces, and portraits, the work in the Doges' Palace, in the Accademia, and the collections of private owners, there must be of this painter's work well-nigh three hundred examples whose authenticity is beyond dispute, while, needless to say, there are plenty of pictures to be found in the collections of dealers and amateurs that have rather more than a suspicion of Robusti's hand, though they can hardly claim to be painted by him alone. Like all other masters Tintoretto had his pupils, and his children and pupils between them would appear to be very largely responsible for some of the pictures that bear his name. To add to the difficulties of the visitor, Tintoretto has suffered more than most men from exposure, neglect, and repainting. The salt-savoured air of Venice is by no means the best in the world for pictures; and candles, though they may save their pious purchasers from many years' suffering in Purgatory, have an awkward habit of smoking and spoiling the altar pictures that stand before them. Candle smoke respects neither madonna nor saint, and though raised with the best intentions, will destroy masterpiece or daub with equal certainty and indifference. In Tintoretto's time piety was more fashionable than art criticism, and his pictures have suffered very much from the devotion they have inspired in the breasts of those to whom candles were a short-cut to salvation. Happily the Scuola of St. Roque, with its countless beautiful works of the master on panel and ceiling and staircase, still preserves a great deal of its original beauty. The Doges' Palace has a splendid collection, including the famous "Paradise" in the Hall of Council, while other apartments in the palace boast specimens of the master's most inspired work. The Royal Palace, and that of Prince Giovanelli, are very rich in the fruit of Tintoretto's labours, while the Academy of Fine Arts from which a part of the pictures given here were taken, holds some of the painter's masterpieces in really favourable positions.

In the Doges' Palace the neck and back of the man who wishes to study Tintoretto must endure constant strain, and the great compositions are so hard to understand that headache often anticipates comprehension, and appreciation gets no chance. The Academy is not too crowded, save at the season of the great American invasion, and there it is possible to enjoy Tintoretto quietly.

PLATE VI.—QUEEN ESTHER FAINTING BEFORE AHASUERUS

(Hampton Court Palace)

Here we have one of Tintoretto's spirited compositions in which he makes no attempt to adapt his costumes to the period of the Bible story. One and all the figures are sixteenth-century Venetians.

The more we study Tintoretto the more his mastery for every branch of his art becomes apparent. His composition is the more marvellous because he had not had the advantage of receiving inspiration from other masters. He carried composition farther than it had gone before, bringing to his aid in that work a certain dramatic instinct that does not seem to have been associated with the painter's workshop before his time. He redeemed Venetian painting from the charge of bad drawing that had been levied against it by the Florentines, and when we come to colour we find that Tintoretto has little or nothing to yield in this department even to Titian himself, and that he gets many of his finest effects from lower tones than those that appealed to his master. Some of his colour effects are less daring, less theatrical, less immediate in their appeal than those of Titian, but when they are understood they are hardly to be less admired, although we have to admit that in many cases they have been restored, and retouched by many well-meaning fools who did not understand the extraordinary delicacy of treatment that gave the canvas its pristine quality. A picture by Tintoretto in which the rich golden brown tints have survived the passages of the years and the hand of the restorer, is at once a thing to wonder at and be grateful for.

Like all great painters Tintoretto had little use for drawings. He did not believe in making elaborate studies; we can learn this from his first work for the Scuola of St. Roque, when he entered into competition with several big painters, and managed to present a finished picture to his startled patrons and competitors in the shortest possible time. Vasari tells the story, how the brotherhood decided to have some "magnificent and honourable work" on the ceiling of the Scuola, and asked Salviati, Zucchero, Paolo Cagliari (Veronese), and Tintoretto to prepare a design. "While the artists were giving themselves with all diligence to the preparations of their designs," writes Vasari, "Tintoretto made an exact measurement of the space for which the picture was required, and taking a large canvas he painted it at his usual speed, without taking any one into his confidence, and fixed it in the place destined to receive it. On the morning when the brotherhood assembled to see the designs and determine the matter, they found that Tintoretto had completed his work, that he had even fixed it in its place. At this they were very angry, saying that they desired designs, and had not commissioned him to do more than prepare one. Robusti replied that this was his method of preparing designs, and that he knew no other, that all designs and models for a work should be executed in this fashion to the end that persons interested might see what would be offered to them, and might not be deceived. Finding the brethren were still displeased, Tintoretto added that if they did not think fit to pay for the work, he would make a present of it to them for the sake of the saint from whom he had received much kindness. The brotherhood could say no more, for they dare not refuse a gift offered to their patron, and so the picture was accepted, and the brethren had to make their peace as best they could with the angry and disappointed competitors."

It would be pleasing to write at length about the work that Tintoretto contributed to the buildings of the brotherhood, but in the appendix to his third volume of the "Stones of Venice," John Ruskin has dealt so completely and so admirably with the master that those who are interested will find all they seek in his pages. In the lower hall are an "Annunciation," an "Adoration of the Magi," an "Assumption of the Virgin," a "Presentation of Jesus," and several others. In the upper hall there is the wonderful masterpiece of "St.

Roque in Heaven," together with many pictures of the great heroes of Bible History, and the "Last Supper" that Velazquez copied. The refectory holds the great "Crucifixion," and eleven panels devoted almost entirely to single figures.

Tintoretto had a hard struggle to become the painter for the wealthy brotherhood, which had already commissioned work from Titian, Giorgione, Schiavone, and other men of light and leading, but when he had once secured a footing he did not lose the confidence of the brethren. They realised that the master was second to none in the honourable ranks of their painters, and indeed the brotherhood is best remembered to-day because it chose Tintoretto to paint so many of its masterpieces. It would have been a pleasant task to reproduce some of these works here, but it would have been impossible to put on a small page, with any hope of conveying a fair idea of their extraordinary fascination, the "Massacre of the Innocents," "Christ before Pilate," the "Crucifixion," or other pictures of that size. It has seemed better on this account to rest content for the most part with single figures, and to emphasise the one aspect of the painter's many merits. His mastery of composition must be left for those who go to Venice or to some other of the cities wherein the work is seen in all its glory.

PLATE VII.—THE RISEN CHRIST APPEARING TO THREE SENATORS

(In the Venetian Academy)

This is a curious work remarkable for the splendid handling of the figure of Christ. The three Senators are so obviously standing for their portraits that they do not interest us.

Some five years would seem to have elapsed between the time when Tintoretto forced his picture of St. Roque upon the astonished brotherhood, and the time when he painted the "Crucifixion" for the Scuola in return for a fee of 250 ducats, becoming thereafter a member of the brotherhood. He worked for them for ten years or more, leaving the question of terms to their judgment, but receiving a very fair price. By the middle of the 'sixties his position in Venice was assured. He was accepted on every hand as a man who honoured the churches and brotherhoods, civil or religious, that employed him. Unlike Titian he was very reliable, and does not seem to have accepted commissions and then to have ignored them because better work came along unexpectedly. His work in the churches is very varied and is scattered throughout Venice. Ridolfi refers to his early pictures in the Church of St. Benedict, but they are not to be found there now. Santa Maria dell 'Orto, which was one of the first to employ his brush, holds his famous "Last Judgment," a composition of singular nobility, painted with great technical skill, and the wonderful imagination that inspired all the painter's efforts. Unfortunately the details on the canvas are not easily seen, and the whole work would appear to have been handed over more than once to the renovator whose tender mercies, like those of the wicked, are cruel. In the same church there are two "Martyrdoms," one of St. Paul or St. Christopher, and another of St. Agnes, and there is the fascinating "Presentation of the Virgin," which ranks side by side with Titian's masterpiece in the Venetian Academy. Tintoretto's colour scheme is more subdued, but the composition is singularly attractive, and the painter's knowledge of perspective, his gift of conveying atmosphere, his skill in handling the human figure in any position have hardly been seen to greater advantage than in this master work. Perhaps because the church Santa Maria dell 'Orto received the artist's earliest work he loved it above all other churches, for it held the vault of the Vescovis and he chose to be buried there. Clearly he was one for whom his wife's family held no terrors. Many other painters figure in this church, which lies well away from the city's main thoroughfares, by the canal Rio della Madonna dell 'Orto. Palma Vecchio is to be seen there and that Girolamo who is said to have acted for Titian when he wished to expel Tintoretto from his workshop. The church also has a "Pieta" by Lorenzo Lotto, and a "Madonna" by Gian Bellini. Tintoretto's burial in the church is recorded on a tablet.

The church of San Cassiano has two or three pictures by Tintoretto, and that of San Francisco della Vigna is said to have another, but it is not to be seen, and the brethren of St. Francis who pace to and fro along the broken-down cloisters can give no information to intruders armed with red guide-books. San Giorgio Maggiore is rich in Tintorettos, and has one or two attractive works by Bassano. A very famous "Last Supper" was painted for this church, but the work will not vie with much that Tintoretto did elsewhere. Santa Maria dei Frari has a beautiful "Massacre of the Innocents." San Marziale has an "Ascension," and two "Annunciations," together with a work that the painter did not live to finish. On the Giudecca in the old Franciscan Church of the Redentore, where a famous water festival is held throughout one night in the summer, there are two splendid examples of the painter's work, and in the church of the Madonna della Salute there is a "Marriage of Cana." This church holds several pictures by Titian and other masters of renown. Santo Stefano is said to have some famous pictures by Tintoretto in the sacristy, but the writer has not seen them.

The list of church pictures is by no means exhausted. It would not be easy to deal with them without giving these pages a suspicious resemblance to a catalogue. The visitor to Venice may be well advised to visit as many churches as he can, and to remember that many a building of little latter-day significance holds priceless work belonging to the sixteenth century. In Florence there are a score or more of Tintoretto's pictures in the galleries of the Uffizi and the Pitti Palace; in the former there is a striking replica of the "Wedding at Cana" in the Venetian church of the Madonna della Salute, but all these have their crowd of admirers; they are catalogued and clearly seen. In Venice, on the other hand, many a church from which the hurried tourist turns aside holds one or more of Tintoretto's masterpieces, and if it is well hung and has escaped the troublesome attentions of restorer and candle-burner, it will well repay quiet study.

The story that a great picture has to tell travels far beyond its own subject-matter, and the quality of that imagination which is associated with all great work is seen in a very high degree in many a church picture by the great Venetian master. Perhaps he owes his heroic achievements to Michelangelo. The full story of his indebtedness has been treated at length by John Ruskin, for whom the painter's work held great attractions; but it may be said, without fear of contradiction, that where a picture has survived its surroundings, the vigour of mind, the breadth of view, the dramatic sense of the painter, his splendid power of seeing the great stories of Old or New Testament in their most dramatic aspect, will satisfy the most critical sense of the onlooker almost as much as the conquest of difficulties in light, shade, foreshortening, composition, and graded tones please the man who has mastered the technicalities of the painter's art.

Looking at Tintoretto's work and remembering that he hardly stirred beyond the limits of the Republic, it is impossible not to reflect upon the chance and luck that beset the lives of men. Tintoretto, with his splendid gifts, his rapid accomplishment, his courteous manner, remains in Venice; his fame suffering because he could see far beyond the limits that beset the view of his great and popular master. Had Tintoretto not been able to see quite so clearly, had he not alarmed contemporary criticism by groping successfully after the first truths of impressionism, he might have been in the fulness of time the court painter of popes and emperors. His splendour might have been diffused throughout Italy; it might have travelled to Spain, then the greatest of all world powers. Titian, for all his extraordinary gifts, had certain conventional limitations. Tintoretto, equally gifted, could see more deeply into the truths that underlie painting, so he did not prosper in like degree. Happily for him he was a man who worked for work's sake, as long as his hands were full and he could labour from morning until night, the pecuniary and social results hardly seemed worth bothering about. We know that Titian, whose income was much larger than Tintoretto's, was loud in his complaints of bad times and inadequate payments, but if Tintoretto complained, Ridolfi has forgotten to record the fact. There is no attempt here to belittle Titian or to praise Tintoretto; each was a man for whom the sixteenth century and its successors must need be grateful. The difference between them was temperamental, and is worth recording, though it is not set down in any spirit of unfriendly criticism.

PLATE VIII.—ADAM AND EVE

(From the Venetian Academy)

This picture, representing Eve in the act of offering the apple to Adam, is remarkable for the beauty of the flesh painting. John Ruskin was moved to express his admiration for it in terms of enthusiasm.

III

It would seem that the pictures for the brotherhood of St. Roque secured for Tintoretto the crowning honour of his life, the commission to bring his brush to the service of the Doges' Palace. It is hardly too much to say that just as the Doges' Palace is the most remarkable monument of the Venetian Republic left in Venice to-day, so Tintoretto's pictures are the most remarkable decorations in the palace itself. There must be fifty or more of them, if we include the Hall of Grand Council, the Hall of Scrutiny, the College, the Entrance and the Passage to the Council of Ten, the Ante-room to the Chapel, the Senate and the Salon of the Four Doors; but the task of painting fifty pictures, stupendous though it may seem, is not realised until we remember the size and quality of some of these works. The "Paradise," for example, in the Council Hall, is more than twenty-five yards long, and is such a work as many a painter would have given the greater part of his life to; but Tintoretto had little more than six years to live when he undertook the work, and there is no doubt that while the brain behind the picture was always his, the hand was sometimes that of his son or one of his pupils.

It may be supposed that most painters, who have reached Tintoretto's age when they received their commission for the Ducal Palace, would have hesitated to begin work on such a colossal scale. They would have felt that the span of their life could hardly stretch much farther, and knowing that much was to be done in the way of portraits and small pictures, would have been content with these. It was characteristic of Tintoretto that he should at once undertake pictures on the largest scale known to painters. Not only did he undertake the work, but he accomplished it.

The student of Tintoretto who finds himself in Venice should, we think, endeavour to leave the Doges' Palace alone until he has watched the painter's development in the various Venetian churches. Then he should study the work done for the brotherhood of St. Roque, and finally should go to St. Mark's to see the crowning achievement of one of the greatest men who ever took a paint-brush in hand. Students of opera will have noticed how a great singer will sometimes keep his voice back until the work is nearly over, in order to put all his energy into the last act, and so leave an impression that will not be forgotten easily. So it was with Tintoretto. He did splendid work in many directions, but saved himself for the last act, and the crowning achievement of his life was reserved for the Doges' Palace. There all the inspiration that had blossomed in the Venetian churches, and budded in the Scuola of St. Roque, came suddenly into flower, and the visitor to the palace will look in vain throughout the civilised world for an equally enduring monument to any one man. Other great artists have left their traces in many cities, but it may be doubted whether Michelangelo and Raphael in the

Vatican have left a more enduring record than Tintoretto gave to the Palace of the Doges. So vast was his achievement, so brilliant was his imagination, that our eyes, trained down to see small things, and unaccustomed to realise the full idea underlying great pictures, tremble before the "Paradise" and "Venice with the Gods and the Doge Nicolo da Ponte," or the "Capture of Zara," or "St. Mark Introducing the Doge Mocenigo to Christ," or the splendid "Descent from the Cross," in the Senate, or the Pagan picture in the Salon of the Four Doors, in which Jupiter gives Venice the Empire of the Sea. Any one of these pictures might have been regarded as the crowning achievement in the life of a very considerable painter. Before them all imagination stops. Certainly Tintoretto was a long time coming into his kingdom, but there could have been few to dispute his supremacy when he arrived.

In 1574 Tintoretto applied to the Fondaco de Tedeschi for a broker's patent, and thus history repeated itself, for it will be remembered that Titian had endeavoured to secure Bellini's place in the great house of the German merchants, and now Tintoretto was supplanting Titian. The application seems to have been quite successful. The house to-day serves as a general post-office, and still shows some slight trace of the frescoes of Giorgione and Titian. There does not seem to be any record of work that Tintoretto did for the German merchants, but the appointment was largely an honorary one as far as the work went, although it brought a certain income to the fortunate owner of the office. Tintoretto had now reached the time when his work could no longer be ignored, and even Florence which looked askance at art in Venice elected the painter a member of its Academy, an honour that was conferred also upon Titian, Paul Veronese, and a few smaller men.

Throughout all the years in which the painter's art was maturing, and the circle of his patrons was widening, he seems to have lived a quiet and uneventful life in Venice, seeking friends in his own circle, labouring diligently in his studio, and never permitting the claims of affairs lying outside his work to tempt him to be idle. A man of happy disposition, with no vices, and no extravagant tastes, he would seem to have found his earning sufficient for his need, and to have been happy in his home life, although we have already recorded the fact upon Ridolfi's authority that like so many other good men Tintoretto was in the habit of telling lies to his wife. Signora Robusti must have been a little trying when she sought to regulate her husband's expenditure, the times of his going out and coming in, and other trifles of the sort that good women delight to take an interest in.

The great grief of Tintoretto's life was happily delayed until 1590, when the well-beloved Marietta, who had been her father's friend and companion for so long, died. The shock must have been a very serious one, for Tintoretto himself was well over seventy, but it does not seem to have diminished his activity. He would appear to have given all his days to his own labour, or the superintendence of the labours of others, and so the years crept on uneventfully for him, until the last day of May 1594 when his strenuous, vigorous, and brilliant career found its closing hour, and those whom he left behind, together with a great concourse of admiring citizens, took him to the tomb of his wife's house in the Church of the Madonna dell 'Orto, which he had enriched with so much fine painting. His daughter, having predeceased him—as we have seen, she was a portrait painter, and her father's dearest friend—his son Domenico carried on the family work, and completed his father's commissions, but neither brain, nor hand, nor eye could compare with those that were now at rest, and the younger Tintoretto makes small claim upon the attention of artist or historian.

So a very great man passed out of the life of Venice, and for a brief while his fame slumbered, but in years to come great artists, Velazquez foremost among them, made the great city of the Adriatic a place of pilgrimage for his sake. His influence, travelling on another road, extended as far as Van Dyck. We have already traced the descent to the modern school of impressionism, but he would be a bold man who would say that the influence of Tintoretto is exhausted, or holds that he has nothing to teach the twentieth century. His light will hardly grow dim as long as his painting has a claim upon the attention of civilised men.

The plates are printed by BEMROSE DALZIEL, LTD., Watford
The text at the BALLANTYNE PRESS, Edinburgh

Milton Keynes UK
Ingram Content Group UK Ltd.
UKHW011721190424
441445UK00017B/335